Twei
Mastering the Difficult Conversation
JOURNAL

By Leslie C. Fiorenzo, CoachWithLeslie.com

©2019 Wyoming, MI 49509

INTRODUCTION

This Journal is the next step in mastering the difficult conversation. It is designed to turn what you have learned and will be learning for the next twenty-one days into a HABIT. That is, it is an automatic way of dealing with teams and direct reports.

The first section introduces the D.A.R.E. Process for Resolution Management and includes 3 Massive Mistakes Even Savvy Managers Make When Dealing With Difficult Employees, Mastering the Difficult Conversation. I would like to have a magic wand for you to wave over the party(s) in question to change their behavior and make everything great. I don't. What I do have is some practical advice for you to use, assuming you *want* to take steps to prepare yourself to masterfully resolve the issue(s) which ultimately makes life better -- for you and for your direct reports. *What do I mean by better?* Better being defined: *as repairing − or leaving the relationship.* Of course ultimately the choice will be yours.

The second section is your Daily Journal with twenty-one daily lessons. Select a lesson each day, in any order you choose, and after you read it, read it again. Then write out your insights and questions based on the lesson. Now you are taking the first section of this book and are adding vital content to have you grow as a leader who is an expert at managing those 'difficult conversations.'

PART I

Introducing the D.A.R.E. Process for Resolution Management

Allow me please to "DARE" (Daily Actions for Reaching Excellence) you, the manager or supervisor, to be open to first change *your* current perspective on conflict resolution in the workplace! This report   is written to provide you practical and effective concepts to be the master of conflict resolutions. I recommend you review these concepts several times a week until you feel like you *own* them.

At that point you will likely want to move on to the twenty-one factors in the DARE Process, learned over twenty one days. *Why twenty-one days?* Because research demonstrates it takes twenty-one days to create a new habit ... and excellence is a new habit. [I recommend you repeat the DARE twenty-one day process every quarter each year. Why? Because we learn through repetition and you are always growing ... what you glean from reading and journaling the next quarter will likely be quite different than the one before. And so it goes].

As you read, please keep the following in mind: In the basement of Westminster Abbey, the Anglican Bishop's tombstone read this paragraph:

"When I was young and free and my imagination had no limits,
I dreamed of changing the world.
As I grew older and wiser I discovered the world would not change -
So I shortened my sights somewhat and decided to change only my country,
But it too seemed immovable.
As I grew into my twilight years, in one last desperate attempt,
I settled for changing only my family, those closest to me,
But alas, they would have none of it.
And now I realize as I lie on my deathbed, if I had only changed myself first,
Then by example I might have changed my family,
From their inspiration and encouragement I would
Then have been able to better my country,
And who knows,
I might have even changed the world."
Best wishes for success,
Leslie

Three Massive Mistakes Even Savvy Managers Make
When Dealing with Difficult Employees
Mastering the Difficult Conversation

MISTAKE #1: WE LISTEN WITHOUT HEARING WHAT'S REALLY BEING SAID

How many times did someone come to our office with a problem, and we think — *I've heard this before!* Or, *Oh no not this again!* Our assumptions about this difficult situation will likely *limit* our ability to grasp what the other person is feeling. We may hear the words, yet ... *do we really understand the feeling behind what they are saying?*

Listening for understanding takes time, and *time* is a precious commodity. In the day to day "busyness" of our lives it can be challenging to stop and listen.

There are so many things demanding our attention. Think about the last time someone listened to you yet failed to understand what you really said and intended. *How did that make you feel?* Probably not very good. Now put yourself in the shoes of the person who wants *you* to listen. If they leave the conversation and don't feel heard and understood, it impacts how they feel about the entire organization, and themselves. The employee will now complain that *they* don't care. "They "in this case represents more than just the HR department — it's the entire organization.

When you practice your listening skills, you will find people are satisfied and walk away feeling good. Here are some phrases you can use in your listening conversation.

- Tell me more about that?
- Why do you say that?

And of course, it's more than just using the phrases; it's the intent behind the phrases. This is the time for humility. Avoid make judgments about what the person is saying. Avoid giving advice unless the individual talking asks for it.

If you are a Star Trek: Voyager fan you may remember episode involving the Collective. The episode portrayed Borg cube as a horrible place where everyone was melded into one common consciousness, no one was allowed a different opinion, or to be independent in any way. At the end of the episode the Borg children, abandoned by the Collective, discover their names and true identities and all is well. US citizens have an independent nature. While that can be of benefit, failing to recognize the connection we have with others can cause problems. When we fail to listen at a deep level, we may dismiss the other individual as unimportant or not worth our time. We are all connected; when we dismiss someone as unimportant, we miss the opportunity to connect.

We must recognize it is the whole person that shows up for work and as a result, we are unable to separate the home person from the work person.

The heart of the person before you is a mirror; see there your own form
– Shinto version of the Golden Rule.

Try this ... take out a clean sheet of paper, wad it up in your hand, spit into it, throw it on the ground and step on it, grind it into the ground with your foot. Now, pick it up, gently unfold it, spread it out and say, *"I'm sorry."* No matter how many times you say *I'm sorry* the paper will never return to its original state. We cannot remove the wrinkles or the dirt. So it is with the way we treat people at the onset that is critical. We can say I'm sorry over and over yet the damage we cause by treating them with disrespect may never go away.

MISTAKE # 2 – WE FAIL TO RECOGNIZE THE STRESS

In today's world of *work* we are hiring people for their intelligence, not just their brawn. This means we want people to be able to use their pre-frontal cortex to problem solve and *think about* their work. When we are forced to work with someone we perceive as difficult, our prefrontal cortex is high-jacked by our amygdala, the part of the brain that triggers the *flight or fight stress response.*

The amygdala and hippocampus play significant roles in how we humans handle stress. The amygdala is an almond shaped structure deep in the brain that is believed to be a communication hub between the parts of the brain that process incoming sensory signals and the parts that interpret these signals. It can alert the rest of the brain that a threat is present and trigger a stress response. The emotional memories storied in the central part of the brain may sound like this: the last time you had an encounter with this person it turned out badly, danger, danger don't interact with them again! Our Prefrontal cortex is the part of the brain where all creative thought and problem solving take place. You come to a team meeting and you are face to face with that difficult person. Your flight or fight response kicks in and its downhill from there.

Team work is required in organizations today. The actions of one team member may trigger the stress reaction in another. This can happen and almost go unnoticed expect for the person having the stress response. It may show up in physical ways, like an upset stomach or headache. Or it may show up in behaviors; people may fail deliver on their promises. Here is an example. Sometimes it's the words people use to express themselves.

A young man who belonged to a group of volunteers working to complete a project reacted negatively to another volunteer because they often used the word **exclusive** to describe her part in the process. The word **exclusive** showed up 'like nails on the chalk board' to this young man. Every time this woman, his fellow volunteer and someone he needed to work with to accomplish the overall mission of the group, used the word exclusive, he could feel himself getting upset. One day he asked me *if I was bothered by her and how exclusive she was.* "No," I said, and after a conversation, I suggested he approach her in a calm, humble manner and have a conversation. He did. He later told me she had no idea that using the word exclusive was off putting to him yet she could tell by his response to her that something was wrong. She was glad he shared that with her and she was willing to change her language.

MISTAKE #3 - WE HOPE IT WILL GO AWAY ON ITS OWN

Time, in and of itself, never solved a problem. The longer we let a situation go unaddressed, the longer it festers. Like a slow moving infection, it will eventually spread to all parts of the body. Ignore a problem employee situation and it will spread and impact the entire team. It's been my experience that the longer we ignore a situation, the worse it gets. Have a PLANNED conversation.

Now it's time to prepare ourselves to overcome these mistakes for ourselves. Then we are able to better master conflicts in our teams and with our direct reports. This preparation is designed to have you become acutely aware of being the observer and objective when managing conflict between others.

12 Steps to Prepare for the 'conversation'

1. Gather in advance data and documents you need to review with the individual(s).
2. Think through the interaction; see yourself conducting a successful and meaningful conversation with the person to resolve the issue. You are not looking for the admission of guilt -

both parties are at fault. You want to reach agreement on performance expectations.

3. Visualize the conversation going smoothly, without raised angry voices, tears or other emotional outbursts.
4. Limit your opening statement to a description of their behavior. Avoid starting with a question, such as 'What do you think you're doing?' Rather, describe what you have observed. 'Harold, you've missed the last three deadlines for your part of the project.'
5. Acknowledge the effect their behavior is having on you, the team, the department or the entire company. 'The deadline with our client is this Friday. If the work is not finished, the entire project will be in jeopardy.
6. Articulate or spell out clearly the change that needs to take place. 'I need the reports on my desk by 3:00 p.m. If you are not able to complete the task, I need to know about it so we can work something out.'
7. Then, be quiet and wait for their response.
8. Name the consequence. Identify what will happen if the agreed upon change does not take place. Just like physics, where every action has an equal and opposite re-action, every behavior has a consequence.
9. Create clear expectations, time lines and benchmarks.
10. Schedule a follow-up meeting and keep the meeting. If you expect the other person to follow-though, you must as well.

11. Evaluate the meeting. Did the conversation go as planned? What will you do differently in the future?
12. If using this method doesn't produce a change in the person's behavior, it may be time to enlist the help of a consultant, coach or counselor — professional help.

Overcoming the Three Massive Mistakes

1. UNDERSTANDING THE POWER OF THE FUD FACTOR

Several years ago, I was part of a team that meets annually for two days to complete a process called **Best Year Yet**. During our 2007 meeting, the question was asked, *"How do we limit ourselves?"* Joe Ward, a team member at the time, eloquently described what he calls **the FUD Factor: Fear, Uncertainty and Doubt.** Joe said, "We limit ourselves because we have fear, uncertainty and doubt. That is what really holds people back. I believe everything in our lives that we fail to complete can be traced back to one of the three — Fear, Uncertainty or Doubt."

When we allow *Fear Uncertainty and Doubt (FUD)* to take over even one facet of our life, we cannot move forward. We get 'stuck.' We are 'paralyzed.' We have anything **but** our best year. In his book *Good to Great*, Jim Collins states that *good is the enemy of great*. Many people and organizations do good work. Because we are being 'good,' we don't take the steps to bring it to great. Each of us has some FUD in our lives that keeps us from moving forward and accomplishing great things.

Each day take one step in the direction of your goal. Each step will begin to change your perception and your reality. Every biography I've read on successful people has had this common theme; everyday they took small steps to reach their goals. They remained focused on the goal and although they encountered obstacles in their paths, they were persistent and eventually succeeded. Nothing stopped them. Did they have the FUD Factor? Absolutely. They simply overrode it and continued putting one foot in front of the other toward their goal and their greatness.

"To become different from what we are, we must have some awareness of what we are." - Eric Hoffer

2. BECOME AWARE OF CURRENT SOCIETAL PROGRAMMING

We live in a society programmed for instant gratification. We want it NOW. We want to lose the extra weight ... overnight. We want to have a million dollars in the bank ... tomorrow. We want our children or our spouse or our parents to improve *today*. TV ads encourage us to swallow a pill or down a drink and we will be instantly thin, sexy and happy. There are no quick fixes, no instant transformations. The only place success comes before work is in the dictionary! Successful people know it is the work done consistently over a period of days, weeks, months and years that allowed them to reach their goal.

Daring to change your tune requires learning techniques and strategies that are applied each and every day, to move you from the bottom to the top.

3. BEGIN TO CHANGE YOUR FOCUS

So, why change your focus? **Because you get what you focus on.** We've all had "one of those days," when we get a late start, traffic is snarled, the boss barks at us, the kids are naughty, our co-worker is surly and uncooperative, we get a parking ticket, and the list goes on and on. The more we focus on what is wrong, the more things go wrong! When we continue to think about how bad, wrong, or unfair things are ... we get more of the same. When we change our thoughts and our focus to what we are grateful for and what makes us happy, the result will match our thoughts. Try it! Use this report as a tool to help you change your focus. Carry it with you and refer to it often.

Many books and articles have been published about goals and goal setting. The common directive is to write out your goals. Bob Pike, founder of the Bob Pike Group and expert trainer, says, *"If you think it, ink it."* If our goals are not written down, they are described as hopes, dreams and wishes...but not goals. Just like a point on the map, our goal becomes our destination.

If you are planning a road trip from one point to another, you would start by looking at a map. You would find the distance between the two cities and calculate how far you want to drive each day to reach the destination. If you had a two-week vacation, you might take three days to drive and stop and see sights along the way. If you were driving to reach a loved one in the hospital, you would likely drive straight through, day and night, until reaching your destination. So it goes with our goals. They are the map that serves as the guide in your journey. You determine your travel time. Experts agree, in order to change your life for the better and create the life of your dreams, you must take focused steps toward your goals each day.

Jack Canfield, co-author of the *Chicken Soup for the Soul* series, advises we do something every day that gets us *out of our comfort zone*. The challenge we have is that our brain *likes* comfort. Our brain likes sameness. The good news is we can retrain our brain. Take one small, uncomfortable step today, then another tomorrow, then one more the next. In twenty-one days of this practice, you will be amazed at the steps you've taken. The next time you think to yourself, *"Hey you can't do that! Who do you think you are? "* Avoid listening! Go for it anyway! Step into and through the limits you've placed on yourself.

4. MAKE A DECISION

All legendary heroes have a vision. The framers of the U.S. Constitution had a vision; a country where people could worship as they choose, free from government interference. Martin Luther King had a vision; he called it a *dream*. He saw a country free from racial prejudice. "*I have a dream that my four little children will one day live in a nation where they will not be judged by the color of their skin, but by the content of their character. I have a dream today!*" What is your vision? Maybe you've heard the term – Big Hairy Audacious Goal. "BHAG" was proposed by James Collins and Jerry Porras in their 1996 article entitled *Building Your Company's Vision*. A BHAG (pronounced BEE-hag) is a form of vision statement "*...an audacious 10-to-30-year goal to progress towards an envisioned future.*"

"*A true BHAG is clear and compelling, serves as a unifying focal point of effort, and acts as a clear catalyst for team spirit. It has a clear finish line, so the organization can know when it has achieved the goal; people like to shoot for finish lines.*" -Collins and Porras, 1996

Whatever term you want to use, you need to **decide** what you want and move faithfully in the direction of your dreams. Our dreams, our quest, our vision, our BHAG ... all give us a focal point; something to aim for. It creates a desire within us. A vision inspires. A vision keeps us centered. Without a vision we become confused. We take no action when we are confused. As the Cheshire Cat so aptly told Alice on her journey through Wonderland, *"When we don't know where we are going any road will take us there."*

Step 1: Decide What You Want. Be specific and detailed. Write in the present tense.

Instead of writing "I will" or "I want..." start your goal statements with the words "I am." Review your goal statements daily. Brian Tracy, internationally acclaimed speaker and author, advises *we become what we think about*. Since we have the ability to choose our thoughts, a written record of your goals will help keep you on track and make progress each day. Keep this written record with you and refer to it first thing each morning, again at mid-day, and then in the evening.

There is a story about five frogs sitting on a log overlooking a pond. The frogs decide to jump off. *How many end up in the water?* None of them because all they did was <u>decide</u>. Not one of them took action. Action, therefore, is the next logical step.

Step 2: Take Action

You may be familiar with the Chinese proverb – *a journey of 1000 miles begins with a single step.* Take a step each day in the direction of your dreams. We can get bogged down our busy lives; our work, family, recreation, all of the everyday tasks we need to manage and perform. This "busyness" can keep us from our dreams. Take the time; make the time to take one step each day to pursue your dream.

Step 3: Document Your Actions

The palest ink is better than the best memory. This report was developed to help you record each step of the way. Anthony Robbins says *if life is worth living it is worth recording.* The only way to review data is if you've captured it in some written form.

You may prefer to write at the end of the day reflecting back on the events that unfolded and planning for tomorrow. Or, you may write notes throughout the day, capturing thoughts as they occur. Some of you will write in the morning. Find the time that is best for you.

Step 4: Evaluate Your Progress

Einstein gave us a description of insanity: *doing the same thing over and over again and expecting different results.* At the end of this twenty-one day period, stop and evaluate. *Are your actions each day taking you closer to your dream?* If not, change what you are doing.

5. START WITH YOUR 'WHY'

In a recent article, sales guru Jeff Gitomer wrote: *"The toughest answers and the most important answers in your life are the ones you have to give yourself: how did you do it or why you didn't get it done."* Many times "it" doesn't get done because we fear the change it will bring. We fear the unknown. We have big dreams and plans and enjoy thinking about them, yet when it comes to doing the actual work to accomplish the goal; we stop and fail to take action.

This happened to me writing this report. It's been on my mind for several years. I started the original version about ten years ago and it sat in my bottom desk drawer until recently when I began to 'feel the calling' to revise and rewrite. I still find it a challenge sometimes to take action to write when I listen to my inner dialogue that says: *No one will want to read what you write. Who do you think you are? You don't have the talent or the resources to make it happen.* You get the idea. Maybe you have the same critical voice stopping you. Change it! I did because you are reading this report! Adopt a mantra that inspires and motivates you toward your goal. I use my personal mantra whenever I get or feel 'stuck.' When I get stuck I repeat it over and over to myself.

Find a mantra that works for you. Repeat it over and over anytime you are not taking the action you planned to take and even when you are. Repetition is the key. The same principle applies to taking action. As Nike says – *Just do it!*

Simon Sinek advises we start with *why*. Why is the purpose, the cause or the belief that inspires you to do what it is you do. This can be a challenging question — knowing your why, as many are working to get a paycheck based on what we studied in school; however, it may not allow us to use our gifts and talents and do what we love and are meant to do. If you feel stuck in your job, unhappy with what you do every day, you can choose to change. Ask yourself, as Gitomer advises why *isn't this getting done?* Chances are you will find you are likely afraid of the result.

My advice is to start by identifying your WHY. It will give you a direction and purpose for this journey. It will be a guidepost to come back to when you hit a bump in the road. Take a few minutes now to write in your personal journal the answer to these questions:

- Why do you want to make a change?
- Why is this important to you?

6. WHAT'S YOUR VISION?

Japanese Proverb – Vision without action is a daydream. Action without vision is a nightmare.

As you finish reading this, I invite you to keep these ideas in mind as you continue your journey with D.A.R.E. Process for Resolution Management: Twenty-One Days: Twenty-One Lessons and Journal.

"People often tell me motivation does not last and I tell them bathing doesn't either. That is why I recommend it daily." - Zig Ziglar

Put this Latin proverb in a place where you can refer to it often: ***the imagination exercises a powerful influence over every act of sense, thought, reason, -- over every idea.***

Our imagination is an influential tool that can be our greatest asset to us or do harm. When we have to work with someone we can't tolerate, our imagination gets in the way of problem solving. It creates worst case scenario stories that we tell ourselves over and over again. In other words, we worry about what is going to happen. And worry has no benefits.

How do you want your life to be different? What new habit do you want to instill? What old habit do you want to eliminate? Take a few minutes and write out the answers so you can refer to them on your journey. They can become your map, your guide, the place you go back to when you get stuck.

PART 2
The JOURNAL

Twenty-One Lessons for
Mastering the Difficult Conversation
Contents

Stop Complaining
Be Persistent
Embrace Change
Avoid Being 'Too Busy'
Choose Excellence over Perfection
Give up the Need to be Right
Communicate Expectations
Create Peace
Watch Your Language
Choose Your Words Wisely
Choose Response over Reaction
Combine High Tech with High Touch
Are You Involved or Committed?
Find the Good
What Are You Willing to Give?
Shake It Off
Adopt an Attitude of Gratitude
Take Action
Be Yourself
Will You Be Better
Celebrate

1.   **Stop Complaining**

The Story:
I live in Michigan and it gets cold here in the winter. As I write this we've had a week of cold and snow. Temperatures have been in the teens during the day, single digits at night and a below zero wind chill. A friend of mine posted a line about how much she despised the weather on her social media page earlier in the week. She went on to say, "Please don't tell me I live in Michigan and should expect it. I don't want to hear it!" I chuckled. Then I got a little sad for her and all the energy she was using to complain about the weather, something she cannot control.
There is not a thing any of us can do to change the weather.

The Lesson:
The next time you catch yourself 'ready' to complain, regardless of what or why, stop and ask yourself two questions.
1. *What can I control?* (Hint: you control your response.)
2. *How can I reframe or reword what I am thinking to respond in a different manner?*

Admittedly, this is hard to do in the moment so we need to give it some thought and practice as often as we 'catch ourselves' ready to complain. As a young girl, I attended Camp Fire Girls camp each summer. We sang a song that went something like this: *It's a poor man who can't see the beauty in the sun and the wind and the rain. And it's a sad man who can love his neighbor and always finds cause to complain.* I am grateful that *I'm not a poor man I'm not a sad man!* I have the sun and the moon and wind the rain and I never lack for good company. The lyrics remind us that there is beauty all around us. We only need to look for it. We get what we focus on. We have a choice and the challenge is to make the choice that brings joy. To make the choice that brings happiness.

Journal Entry:
Create a list of two situations you complain about most frequently. Then reframe (write out) a new (positive) way to think about it.
EXAMPLE: A compliant about weather.
Oh, no it's raining again! That means an umbrella, boots and lots of traffic on the roads! Reframe: I remember the drought last summer when all the lawns were brown, there were no flowers in bloom. When it finally did rain, the next morning everything was bright and green and thriving. Rain is a good thing. Then check in on how you 'feel.'

Lesson 1. Stop Complaining Date: _____

2. Be Persistent

The Story:
Decades ago, when most of the USA was rural, a young man lived on a farm and dreamed of a better life. He wanted to work in New York City. He didn't know anyone in New York, but that did not stop him. He walked to the library in the nearest town and located the addresses of every department store he could find. He then began a letter writing campaign. With a goal of fifteen letters a week, it took him twenty weeks to write to the three hundred department stores he originally identified. Months went by and he did not receive a response. He was not deterred from his dream. He saved his money, bought a train ticket and left for New York. He had enough money to last one week. If he didn't find a job it was back to the farm. The first department store he stopped at the manager told him yes, he did receive his letter, but it was forwarded to the personnel department at their company headquarters, the young man should go there. When he arrived at the personnel department the manager greeted him warmly and said they had been expecting him. Many of the letters he wrote to this company's individual stores had been forwarded to the personnel office. The young man was hired and went on to have a successful career in New York City.

The Lesson:
There is an old adage in the advertising business: *it takes seven exposures to a product or services before people begin to be aware of the product or service.* In the world of sales the adage: *most sales are made after the seventh follow up call yet most sales people give up after three tries.*
Remember if at first you don't succeed try, try again.

Journal Entry:
List five things you can do to be persistent in reaching your goal.

Lesson 2. Be Persistent Date: _____

_____

_____

_____

_____

_____

_____

3.   Embrace Change

The Story:
Change is the only constant in life, yet most of
the time change is uncomfortable. What new
research is discovering is that our brain likes
sameness. It likes routine and it takes work to
create new thought patterns. The good news is
that it can be done. Our neuro pathways are
much like the ruts left by the wagon trains
headed west. It's been over 100 years since
people took the Oregon Trail west, yet the ruts
created by the wagons are still visible today. At
one time scientists thought your brain did not
grow or change once you reached your twenties.
We now know you can create new connections
in your brain until the day you die. Your brain
can be stronger at eighty then when you were
twenty. We need to be deliberate in our thinking
to create new connections and strengthen our
brain.

The Lesson:
We have the choice to change how we think
about things in any given second.

Journal Entry:

To practice changing how you think about a situation, write down ten words that would describe what's going on in your life and then review your list. Change any negative words into positive, their polar opposite.

EXAMPLE:
Let's say your list includes the words frustrated, irritated, and disappointed. Cross out frustrated and rewrite satisfied; cross out irritated and rewrite soothed; and cross out disappointed and rewrite pleased. Use the positive words in place of the negative words when you think about the situation. This process will allow you to begin to change the way you are seeing the situation. It will retrain your brain to look for the good. Recognize it takes time and consistency to create a change in our behavior. Note any additional insights in your journal.

Lesson 3. Embrace Change Date: _____

4)   Avoid Being 'Too Busy'

The Story:
Imagine getting to the end of your life and discovering a store room of rewards that could have been yours but you were too busy to find them. Too busy to reach out to a friend in need; visit an elderly relative; spend time with your spouse or children; paint a picture; write a book, compose a song. Pay attention to how many times us say, oh I'm too busy.

The Lesson: Beware the excuse "I don't have time!" We all have the same 24 hours in each day. Why do some people accomplish a lot and some accomplish a little. I believe part of the reason is we do not make ourselves a priority. If your best friend asked you for an hour of your time every day for the next week, you'd probably find the time. Be your own best friend and find an hour each day for you. Maybe it is split up over the day, thirty minutes in the morning and thirty minutes in the evening. Make time to meditate, exercise, draw, write, sing, dance, read, whatever it is you enjoy doing that refreshes and renews your mind, body and spirit. In the *Ultimate Edge Program* Tony Robbins recommends starting each day with light exercise, affirmations, and being grateful. By starting our day in such a way it can help keep us calm and focused when plans don't go our way.

Journal Entry:
Note in your Journal every time you say "I'm too busy." Decide what you will do different tomorrow and enter that commitment in your journal as well

Lesson 4. Avoid Being 'Too Busy'

Date: _____

_____

_____

_____

_____

_____

_____

_____

_____

_____

_____

5)   Choose Excellence Over Perfection
The Story:

What is the difference between excellence and perfection? The dictionary defines excellence as 'the fact or state of excelling' and perfection as 'the highest degrees of proficiency, skill or excellence as in an art form'. If we think of the difference between what is means to be in the state of or the highest degree, it is clear we choose excellence. It is something to work toward. Perfection would indicate the finished product. As long as we are alive we are never finished growing and learning; so the pursuit of excellence, not perfection, is what we work toward.

The Lesson:

Business coach and author, Marc LeBlanc, encourages his clients to use the mantra: *Done is better than perfect*. The need to be perfect trips us up and stops us from accomplishing our goals. It is hard to look in the mirror and say I am where I am because of the choices I made yesterday. Maybe one of those choices was to procrastinate because you are not perfect. The truth is we will never be perfect. The truth is we need to take one hundred percent responsibility for the shape of our life. Remember when you point a finger at someone else; four are pointed back at you.

Journal Entry:
What choice can you make today to have a better tomorrow? Enter that into your Journal.

Lesson 5. Choose Excellence over Perfection

Date: _____

6) Give up the Need to be Right
The Story:

I wonder how many squabbles could be avoided if we gave up our need to be right. I have observed this in my husband's family. There are siblings who no longer speak to one another because someone disagreed with the other party. What if I could step into the other's perspective? Can I let go of my way? There is an American Indian proverb that states never criticize a man until you've walked a mile in his moccasins. The Cheyenne say to not judge your neighbor until you walk two moons in his moccasins.

The Lesson:

What problems could we solve if we really listened for understanding and not to make our point? In the book the *7 Habits of Highly Effective People*, Stephen Covey describes two separate dialogues between father and son. The son tells his father he wants to quit school. In the first rendition the father advises the son. The conversation ends with hurt feelings and misunderstanding.

In the second the father listens and questions the son revealing the real reason he wants to quit he failed a class. I've read this two dialogues to a variety of groups over the years and the response is generally the same, no one believes the second dialogue is possible. I think part of this is because the second behavior is not often modeled. I think the other reason is we, as parents, siblings, managers, even best friends, want to be right.

Journal Entry:

What would happen if we could let go of that need? Enter your thoughts in the Journal.

Lesson 6. Give up the Need to be Right

Date: _____

7)   Communicate Expectations
The Story:

I think we get into trouble in our relationships because we fail to communicate our expectations. One day, a few months ago I had an early morning flight. My husband who was not traveling with me agreed to drop me off at the airport. He is not a morning person so consequently doesn't hop out of bed when I call his name. It occurred to me that morning I never shared my expectation about how things should go on this morning. I have assumed that when I call his name he will acknowledge me and get out of bed. He doesn't. He stays in bed for a few minutes and I feel compelled to call his name again and remind him he needs to get going. That morning his response was, *"Have you ever been late and missed your flight?"* I had to admit, he was right; we've never missed a flight because we've arrived late to the airport.

The Lesson:

What are your expectations when it comes to workplace relationships? Have you communicated your expectations to those involved? An easy example is time and attendance. Similar to the situation I described above, what are your expectations about time and have you communicated them?

EXAMPLE: Pretend you are the kind of person who arrives early because you believe if you aren't early ... you're late. Your coworker is the opposite. They show up at the last minute or a couple minutes after the appointed time. What impact this is having on the relationship? Do you get upset and silently seethe or do you talk about it? Time is just one example of a set of expectations that may not always be made clear. There are many other examples such as how people sign an email message or if they use their cell phone in a meeting.

Journal Entry:

Think of a situation where you have a certain expectation. Ask yourself the following questions.

1) How important is this in the entire scheme of things? In other words if the behavior continues, can I overlook it and not let it interfere with our working relationship? If the answer is no, then I need to speak up.

2) If it is important when will you talk to them?

3) Create a script or outline to follow.

4) Practice

5) Have the conversation.

Lesson 7. Communicate Expectations

Date: _____

8) Create Peace

The Story:

In his work, <u>The Awakened Life</u>, Wayne Dyer, tells the story of his sister-in-law's near death experience. She was in a serious automobile accident and was rushed to the operating room. During the surgery she recalls being up in the corner of the room, looking down at the surgical team working on her body. She described being surrounded by a white light and an extreme sense of peace. Since her recovery nothing bothers her. She is the calmest, most easy going, loving person no matter what happens in her life. Wayne advises: We don't have to have this kind of traumatic event happen to us to live this kind of life. The quality of this kind of experience is only available to us through our thoughts, our minds, through our divine connection. We can have the understanding that we are spiritual beings having a human experience. Whatever your religious belief, try not to put the label on it. Exemplify kindness, love, forgiveness, and gentleness.

The Lesson:

You may be familiar with the song lyric, *"Let there be peace on earth and let it begin with me."* Or the Gandhi quote *"Be the change you want to see in the world."* The Bible says to *put on the shoes of peace. What if every step we took, we took with peace?*

Visualize getting dressed for the day and putting on invisible shoes of peace. Maybe think of them as the ruby slippers Dorothy had on in the Land of Oz. Once they were on her feet, she couldn't take them off. *What if we put on ruby slippers of peace every day? Would we be more patient, kind, loving, caring to others? What difference could we make in the world if we walked in peace?*

Journal Entry:
Use the visualization above to change any potential anxiety into perfect peace, then enter your experience in the Journal.

Lesson 8. Create Peace

Date: _____

_____

_____

_____

_____

_____

_____

_____

_____

_____

_____

_____

_____

_____

_____

9)   Watch Your Language

The Story:
Maybe at some point in your young life your parent told you to watch your language. You may have been experimenting with derogatory words you heard from a friend. Maybe you stopped using that word or phrase or maybe you didn't. What is important to realize is the impact our language has on our ability to be all you can be. Our internal voice can move us forward only to stop us in our tracks.

The Lesson:
Listen and begin paying attention to the words you are using. This applies both to our internal voice, which we say to ourselves, and the words we speak out loud to others. *Do you use words like stupid, dumb, inadequate, ugly, fat, or lazy when you refer to yourself? Do you say I can't, won't, should or shouldn't in reference to taking action?* If you want to change your life, you need to change your language. Our universe is full of possibility. Often the only limits are the limits we set on what we can believe or think we can do. Sometimes those limits are given to us by our well-meaning family.

EXAMPLE: Steve Harvey, in his new book, writes about an experience he had with a grade school assignment. He was asked to write about what he would be when he grew up. He wrote he would be on television. The teacher gave him a failing grade. When he questioned her, she asked *"Do you know anyone on television? Is anyone in your family on television?"* He came home and shared the story with his parents. His mother said he needed to re-write the assignment. His father, however, encouraged him and said if he thinks he is going to grow up and be on TV then let him.

The lesson is two-fold. First, our family and other important people in our lives try to protect us from hurt and disappointment. Big dreams, like being on TV or preaching to the world, take big action. Big dreams also require risk and risk could mean failure. As parents we don't want to see our children fail, so instead, we encourage them to play small and stay safe. Second, we allow those limits to sink in and become our reality. We say, Oh I could never do that. Or, I'm too old, I'm too young, I'm not smart enough, I don't have my degree. You get the idea. If you use words the limit you, change your language. *Do you say things like I can't, I won't I don't?* Take the "not" off the words and they become can, will, do.

Journal Entry:
See if you can catch yourself saying these words
and jot down how many times in one day you
stopped yourself. Also enter any insights you
may have during this exercise.

Lesson 9. Watch Your Language
Date: _____

10)   Choose Your Words Wisely

The Story:
When I was young I remember my dad responding to the question *"How are you?"* by saying *fair to middlin' more middlin' than fair*. As a kid I didn't think anything of this reply and as an adult I must admit to using the answer myself. The more I learn about how important positive language is to our health and well-being the more I realize the better response is to *"How are you?"* is GREAT! or, "fabulous," or "fantastic" or any other positive descriptor of happiness.
EXAMPLE: Think about how we respond to the weather. I am not familiar with the tools the meteorologist uses to predict the weather. Every day most of us tune into the weather report. If you travel or send little ones to school it is important information. How many times during the day does our conversation turn to the weather and how good or bad it is. Here is what I find interesting.

The Lesson:
We have no power to change the weather, yet it is often a topic of conversation filled with emotion.

We complain it is too hot, or too cold, or too rainy or too snowy or too whatever! This complaining is a lot like worry. I'm sure you've heard worry is *a lot like rocking in a rocking chair, you are moving but you are not really getting anywhere.* Complaining about the weather is similar; it seems like we are taking action, yet we only control our response. I remember a quote ... something along the lines of – *the snow has no malice or good will, it is simply snow.* It is our interpretation of the snow that makes the difference. Our language therefore can forecast our future. In his book, *The Greatest Salesman In the World*, Og Mandino writes: *Trees and plants depend on the weather to flourish but I make my own weather, yea I transport it with me. If I bring rain and gloom and darkness and pessimism to my customers then they will react with rain and gloom and darkness and pessimism and they will purchase naught. If I bring joy and enthusiasm and brightness and laughter to my customers they will react with joy and enthusiasm and brightness and laughter and my weather will produce a harvest of sales and a granary of gold for me.*

Let me invite you to think about the language you are using to talk about your life. Do you say – I really hate that…. What if you said, I would prefer … Or instead of saying I'm so tired what if you said I need to recharge. Try replacing the works you use: different instead of terrible, unique instead of weird. You get the idea.

Remember the words of Mahatma Gandhi, *"Keep your thoughts positive because your thoughts become your words. Keep your words positive because your words become your behavior. Keep your behavior positive because your behavior becomes your habits. Keep your habits positive because your habits become your values. Keep your values positive because your values become your destiny."*

Journal Entry:

In your own life, can you think of ways you use words routinely that are not positive?

Lesson 10. Choose Your Words Wisely

Date:

11)   Choose Response over Reaction

The Story:
Employees have three needs: physical, financial
and emotional. Most employers address the
physical needs of employees by offering health
insurance and financial needs by offering
disability insurance, life insurance and a
retirement savings option like a 401K or 403B.
The emotional needs maybe be addressed by an
employee assistance program, but utilization is
often low. Many people have told me they view
this as the most underutilized program offered
by an employer. Why? Perhaps it is because we
fail to see how emotions drive our behavior.
American psychologist Albert Ellis developed
Rational Emotive Behavior Therapy (REBT, a
form of psychotherapy and a philosophy of
living he developed in the 1950's). In his work,
Ellis created the ABC model. This simple format
teaches us how our beliefs cause our emotional
and behavioral responses.   It looks like this:
A – stands for Activating event
B – our Beliefs about the event
C – the Consequences or what happens as a
result.
EXAMPLE:
A. Our boss criticizes our work.
B. We believe, *"She is wrong and doesn't know
what she is talking about!"*
C. You become angry.

You can't change the fact that your boss is critical of your performance. You can only change your belief about that event and therefore change your response. If you change your belief you can change the emotion that is created as a result.

Let's say you are open and willing to have a conversation with the boss. You think, maybe the boss has an interesting point and you are willing to listen and dialogue with the boss. Instead of getting angry and defensive, you become calm and curious.

You can insert any life event for A. You cannot change A.

The only power and control you have is over B, your belief about the event.

There was a farmer living in Russia in the late 1800's. He and his son were out plowing the field on a fine spring day. Their horse was hitched to the plow. As they are working, the horse suddenly breaks free from the plow and runs away. The farmer and his son are left to continue their work without the aid of their horse. That night they share their story with their fellow villagers. *"How awful! What terrible luck."* the villagers exclaim. The farmer just shakes his head and says, *"You never know."*

A few days later the horse comes back and brings a friend. A wild horse follows it back to the field where the farmer and his son are working. They capture the wild horse and keep it. That night the villagers again talk about the great luck the farmer has and the farmer just shrugs his shoulders and says, *"You never know."* A few days later as the farmer and his son are breaking the wild horse for farm work; the son is thrown from the wild horse and breaks his leg. Later that evening, as the village gathers together to discuss the events of the day, they bemoan the farmer's bad luck. The farmer's response is, *"You never know."* A few weeks later as the son is in bed recuperating, the Cassocks storm the village and take every eligible young man of fighting age with them except the farmer's son because of his broken leg. As the mourning villagers come together that evening, they are happy for the farmer because his son was left behind, and again proclaim it as a stroke of luck. And of course the farmer says, *"You never know."* The farmer knew, as Ellis taught, it is not the events that shape our feelings but our beliefs about the events that create stress and anxiety or peace and happiness in our lives.

The Lesson:
So here we are in our modern lives often
responding the same way the villagers of over
one hundred years ago did to the events that
happened in their day. We now know it is not
what happens to us but how we interpret and
respond to the events in our lives that make the
difference.

Journal Entry:
Think about an event that happens in your life
where you often respond by getting angry or
upset. Getting cut off in traffic is a great
example. *Do you respond by yelling and screaming
at the other driver because you believe they are stupid
and don't know how to drive? Or do you simply
think, Wow, they must be in a big hurry to have
taken such a risk and calmly continue on your way?*
Identify one common event where you can
change your thinking and watch what happens
to your response.

Lesson 11. Choose Response over Reaction
Date: _____

12)   Combine High Tech with High Touch

The Story:
Before the advent of technology, people gathered together and shared stories. Every culture shares stories shared as a means of entertainment, education, cultural preservation, and instilling moral values. Once radio came into fashion people gathered around to listen. Radio broadcasts included: classical music; information about worldwide events, the news; comedy programs from Abbot and Costello or Burns and Allen; or drama such as the *New Adventures of Sherlock Holmes* with Basil Rathbone. Born in the 1950's, television eventually replaced radio as a medium for storytelling.
Fast forward to the current age and almost everyone has a smart device that displays video as a form of entertainment and education. Technology has done much to improve our lives, yet in many ways *it has created a communication gap*. There is no longer a need to come together and receive information, we can get it on demand any place we can get a signal.

The Lesson:
The mistake we can make is to rely on technology to share our message rather than one to one, face to face communication with the people who are important to us.

If we have information to share, technology is a great tool. When we need to discuss an issue and make a decision using technology has its draw backs.

EXAMPLE: Setting up a place and time to meet is sharing information. Discussing agenda items via e-mail or text message leaves a lot to be desired. It doesn't matter if the conversation is between two people or several; using technology that relies on the written word is dangerous. Too much can be left unsaid or misinterpreted. There are many horror stories of people relying on technology to send a message that would have been best delivered in person. Texting or e-mailing someone that they've been laid off is one example that applies. In my own personal experience I learned of a sibling's serious illness from a Facebook post.

Journal Entry:
Try this yourself and enter your insights into your Journal. Before using technology to communicate information, ask yourself these three questions:
1. Will this information come as a surprise?
2. Will the person have questions about what I'm saying?
3. Am I using technology to avoid a difficult conversation?
Note your insights/results in your Journal following this exercise.

Lesson 12. Combine High Tech with High Touch

Date: _____

_____
_____
_____
_____
_____
_____
_____
_____
_____
_____
_____
_____
_____
_____

13)   Are You Involved or Committed?
The Story:

You've probably heard the story when you have bacon and eggs for breakfast the chicken is involved but the pig is committed. The word commit comes from the term *committere,* "to bring together" and one definition is to pledge (oneself) to a position, or an issue or a question. Involve on the other hand comes from *involvere'* and is defined as to include as necessary circumstance, condition or consequence. *Metaphorically speaking are you involved or committed to your work or your team?*

The Lesson:

Commitment seems much deeper than being involved. When we are involved we work at the surface, commitment requires us to reach in, go deep.

EXAMPLE: A newly appointed director of a department of sixteen is struggling to communicate with one of his staff. They worked together as colleagues before his promotion 6 months ago. Over the past few weeks he notices this employee is avoiding conversation and will only speak when spoken to and no longer contributes at team meetings. The director is frustrated because none of his attempts to discuss the matter with this person have been successful.

He had involved his employee in his effort to repair the relationship, without success. Because he is committed to the success of the department and to their working relationship he brought in an outsider (me) to resolve the issue.

Journal Entry:
Here is the question to ask yourself about work and note this in your Journal. *Are you involved or committed? If you shift from being involved to being committed what difference will that make?*

Lesson 13. Are You Involved or Committed?

Date: _____

14) Find the Good

The Story:
We all face challenges in life. Sometimes they are small like getting everyone ready each day and out the door to school or work. Sometimes they are big like pleasing a difficult customer or deciding which product to launch. Either way, these challenges have a similar component. That is controlling how we think about the challenge. *Do we think it will work or won't it work?* When we focus on the will it can be easier to overcome the problem.

Let's use the example of getting everyone ready in the morning. It starts the night before, choosing outfits, making lunches, getting as much preparation work done so when the alarm sounds there is less to do before you need to leave in the morning.

The same applies to a product launch. Identify the date and backward plan so all the details are discussed and worked out before the deadline. Sometimes the best laid plans go awry. This is when we have to ask ourselves *"What's good?* We don't always know why things happen the way they do. The purpose of asking the question ("What's good?") is to switch our thinking from what was wrong to what is right.

Let's take the beginning of our day as an example. We have lunches made and ready to go. We have the table pre-set for breakfast. Clothes are chosen and waiting. In the morning your little one is cranky and uncooperative, so the day doesn't start as planned. Or you are ready the leave and the car won't start. You are delayed and arrive late for work. Ugh! You think that the day is a disaster already.

The Lesson:
Instead of focusing on what went wrong, ask yourself to think of three good things that did happen. One good thing might be that the lights worked and the water came out of the faucet when you turned on the shower and there was food to eat. When we ask what's' good, even when the answers are simple and things we often take for granted, we begin to switch our thinking and retrain our brain to look for the positive. We can adopt this practice to the end of our day or the end of a meeting or the end of a failed project.
Journal Entry:

Before you fall asleep, write in your journal three good things that happened the day you opt to read this lesson. Relive the good feelings that came from the experience. At the end of a meeting, ask each participant what they liked best about the experience. When the project is done focusing on what went right can allow you to build momentum to carry you into the next project.

Lesson 14. Find the Good
Date: _____

15)   What are you willing to give?

The Story:
At the beginning of the book there is a quote by
Anthony Robbins: *Some of the biggest challenges in
relationships come from the fact that most people
enter a relationship in order to get something: they're
trying to find someone who's going to make them feel
good.*

The Lesson:
In reality, the only way a relationship will last is
if you see your relationship as a place that you
go to give, and not a place that you go to take. If
you've ever walked on a forest trail you've
probably seen the sign: *Take nothing but pictures,
leave nothing but footprints.* In other words don't
take any of the wild plants or animals with you
and don't leave your garbage or trash on the
ground. We can take this analogy to our
workplace relationships.

First, avoid spreading trash. Stop using judgment words in your conversation. Words like lazy, careless, or stupid, can have an adverse impact the message we want to send. Second avoid taking the interaction with you into the future. Every interaction can have a memory. At the end of the day, while we sleep, our brain goes to work sorting and categorizing our experiences and putting them into a place we can access. If we dwell on what happened it is more likely to stick with us. Journaling can be an effective tool release the experience and shift our focus.

Journal Entry:
What are you willing to give to the relationship? Maybe it's a simple as a smile. Answer this question: *How can I interact with this person and leave them better than they were before?*

Lesson 15. What are you willing to give?

Date: _____

16)   Shake It Off

The Story:
There is a story of a farmer who had a donkey. One day the donkey fell into a deep pit that was once a well. The farmer summoned his neighboring farmers to help assess the situation. All the farmers agreed the best thing to do was fill the hole and bury the donkey. After all he had lived a good long life and there was no way to rescue the donkey. So they picked up their shovels and began to fill the hole. You can imagine the donkey's surprise when those first shovels full of dirt hit him. He started shaking and kicking and braying. More dirt kept falling and he kept shaking of the dirt and stepping on it. This went on minute after minute, hour after hour. The farmers kept shoveling dirt into the hole and the donkey kept shaking it off and stepping off. After a few hours the donkey stepped up and out of the hole. When faced with the difficult situations in our life we need to remember to shake it off and step up.

The Lesson:

One way to do this is to find something humorous about the situation or something to laugh at in general. A friend experiencing chemo recently told me that we cannot laugh and be in pain and the same time, it's physically impossible. How interesting!

Norman Cousins proved this to be true. He healed himself using laughter. What a lesson for each of us. Search for ways to add laughter into your day, especially in the face of a challenge. Listen to your favorite comedian on a CD or on YouTube. Read the laughter pages in Reader's Digest. It may take a little work, but the effort is worth is.

Journal Entry:
Enter in your journal the method you will use to laugh, shake it off and step up.

Lesson 16. Shake It Off   Date:

17) Adopt an Attitude of Gratitude

The Story:
We have much to be thankful for each and every day. When we go to work every day and face a difficult co-worker or frustrating boss adopting an attitude of gratitude can be a challenge. It is worth the effort. The following words by John F Kennedy are particularly helpful when we choose to assume this stance, "*As we express our gratitude, we must never forget that the highest appreciation is not to utter words, but to live by them.*"

The Lesson:
It is not the creation of the list that makes the difference. It is getting in touch with how the act of being grateful makes us feel and how we act on that feeling.

Journal Entry:
Start a practice of gratitude by writing down at the end of the day, three to five experiences you are grateful for that day.
Or you can speak them out loud to your family at the dinner table in the evening. Or create a practice at your staff meeting by sharing what you appreciate about your work or your team.

Anecdote:
Often at the end of my presentations I will have an audience member come up to me and share this powerful method.
At the top of a piece of paper each person writes their name. They then pass the paper to the left. The person receiving the paper writes something they appreciate about the individual whose name is at the top of the paper. Then the paper is passed to the left again and the next person repeats the process, writing something they appreciate about the individual whose name is at the top of the page. The paper is passed and each person in the group writes until the paper is returned to its owner, the person whose name is at the top of the page.

The last person to share this experience with me told me how honored she felt by the words written by her colleagues and she didn't realize how much people appreciated what she did until she saw it in writing.

Lesson 17. Adopt an Attitude of Gratitude
Date: _____

18)   Take Action

The Story:
It is easy to live in our head and think about moving forward on a project or having a conversation than it is to take action to move the process forward. Yet, action, is where it's at, it's the only place we can make our dreams a reality.

The Lesson:
 The more time we spend in our heads thinking about how bad it is or how it won't work or what a jerk the other person is the less time we have to take action. To date in this journey you've been doing a lot of thinking and writing. Now take action on those thoughts and words. In his first book, *The Greatest Salesman in the World*, Og Mandino wrote an entire chapter on action entitled: I Will Act Now.

Journal Entry:
What action will you take today on your thoughts and words?

Lesson 18. Take Action   Date: _____

19)   Be Yourself

The Story:
Lets' start with a couple of statics: ten percent of the people you meet won't like you and life is ten percent what happens to you and ninety percent how you respond to what happens. *What is the common denominator?* The ninety percent.

The Lesson:
There will always be critics. There will always be people who focus on what's wrong with you or what you can't do. Focus on the people who are on your side. Focus on the people who support you. Spend your time with people who love you. Avoid the Nay Sayers and the doom and gloomers. Every person in history has faced self-doubt. Avoid listening to that negative voice inside your head and the negative voices of others.   We are all here on this earth for a reason and it is our job to discover and live out that purpose. Every day we must live connected to our purpose.

Journal Entry:
Take some time and write out the answers to the following question. Imagine you are celebrating your eightieth birthday.

All your family and friends are gathered with you. *What will they be saying about your life?* The challenge before you is to live each day from now until that birthday so those words will be true. Reflect on this each morning when you wake up. This will set you headed in the direction of your goal.

Lesson 19. Be Yourself   Date:

20)   Will You Be Better?

The Story: In a kingdom far away, there lived a chef and his daughter. The chef was known far and wide for the wonderful food he would create and serve at the king's parties. His daughter was known far and wide because she was a constant complainer. Nothing was ever right. One day, when his daughter turned sixteen, the chef brought her into his kitchen and told her to sit on a stool. *"Daughter, watch!"* he commanded.

The daughter did as she was told and observed her father as he put 3 pots on the stove. He filled each pot with water and lit the fire under each one. In the first he put some potatoes, in the next he put some eggs and in the third he put some coffee beans. He let the water come to a boil and turned the fire down to a simmer. The daughter because her father rarely asked her into his kitchen sat silently and observed. After 20 minutes had passed her father gave her a spoon and asked her to inspect each one of the pots. In the pot with the potatoes she found them soft to the touch, the eggs were of course hard boiled and the coffee beans were now a delicious brew.

The chef turned to his daughter and said, *"The events that occur in our life are much like the boiling water in the pot. In the case of the potatoes, they were hard going in the water, now they are soft. The eggs were fragile when they went in the water and now they are hard. But the coffee beans transformed the water into something different, some would say better. You have the same choice, my daughter. You can let the events of your life make you hard, or soft, or change you into something new and better."*

The Lesson:
So it is with each of us.

Journal Entry:
Think about the events that occurred in the last 24 hours. *Did they soften you? Harden you? Or transform you?* Enter and create a plan for transformation. The next time you face the same situation how can you let it make you better?

Lesson 20. Will You Be Better?

Date: _____

_____

_____

_____

_____

_____

_____

_____

_____

_____

_____

_____

21) Celebrate

Every culture has days for celebration. Many families come together to celebrate events. Find a way to celebrate what you've accomplished on this 21 day journey.

Our 21 day journey has come to a close and I will invite you to keep these ideas in mind as you continue your journey;

"People often tell me motivation does not last and I tell them bathing doesn't either. That is why I recommend it daily." - Zig Ziglar

Put this Latin proverb in a place where you can refer to it often: *the imagination exercises a powerful influence over every act of sense, thought, reason, -- over every idea.* Our imagination is an influential tool that can be our greatest asset to us or do irreparable harm. When we have to work with someone we can't stand our imagination often gets in the way of problem solving. It creates worst case scenario stories that we tell ourselves over and over again. In other words we worry about what is going to happen. And worry has no benefits.

Journal Entry:

Now that you have completed this Journal once, it is ideal to start again!

How do you want your life to be different in the next 21 days, and the next and the next? What new habit do you want to instill? What old habit do you want to eliminate? This entry will become your map, your guide, the place you go back to when you get stuck.

Lesson 21. Celebrate

Date:

ABOUT THE AUTHOR

Leslie C. Fiorenzo founded CoachWithLeslie.com in 2019 after becoming a certified 5 in 5 performance coach with IPV Consulting. She is Director of Employee Assistance Center, West Michigan's oldest provider of employee assistance program services. She has over 25 years' experience as a human resources professional working in the automotive, distribution, and packaging industries. In April of 2014 Leslie and EAC partnered with Anna Maravelas and her company Thera Rising and became certified to present their flagship seminar the Self Defeating Habits of Otherwise Brilliant People®. From 2005 to 2012 Leslie taught human resources, business and marketing courses as an adjunct faculty member at Davenport University. From 2003 until 2011 she was an independent consultant with Business Network International (BNI) the world's largest referral organization and presented to hundreds of sales professionals and small business owners on how to get the most from their membership.

If you are a manager or supervisor struggling in your organization, I would like to short cut your success in mastering conversations with difficult employees with a review of your current process. I encourage you to contact me at leslie@coachwithleslie.com.

Contact Information:
Phone: 616.490-5222
Email: leslie@coachwithleslie.com
Website: www.coachwithleslie.com
LinkedIn: https://www.linkedin.com/in/lesliefiorenzo

Made in USA - Kendallville, IN
1063880_9781655540622
03.27.2020 0825